I0821500

THE BIRD IN THE STILLNESS

FOREST DEVOTIONALS

Joe Rosenblatt

The Porcupine's Quill

Library and Archives Canada Cataloguing in Publication

Rosenblatt, Joe, 1933–, author
The bird in the stillness : forest devotionals / Joe Rosenblatt.

Poems.
ISBN 978-0-88984-394-3 (paperback)

1. Nature--Poetry. I. Title. Title: Forest devotionals.

PS8535.O763B52 2016 C811'.54 C2016-900616-6

1 2 3 • 18 17 16

Published by The Porcupine's Quill, 68 Main Street, PO Box 160, Erin, Ontario NOB 1TO. http://porcupinesquill.ca

Readied for the press by Chandra Wohleber.

Represented in Canada by Canadian Manda Group.
Trade orders are available from University of Toronto Press.

We acknowledge the support of the Ontario Arts Council and the Canada Council for the Arts for our publishing program. The financial support of the Government of Canada through the Canada Book Fund is also gratefully acknowledged.

In Memoriam
Gwendolyn MacEwen

Table of Contents

Mother Nature Was Far Sexier

For over fifty years Joe Rosenblatt has been writing about the natural world, beginning in 1960 with anthropomorphized bumblebees hitting on the marigolds at Toronto's Allan Gardens as they worked the cross-pollinating day shift. Moving further up the evolutionary ladder, a suite of bat poems followed and, later in the eighties, an obsession with both freshwater and ocean fish.

Casting an artificial dry fly on the waterway of the Little Qualicum River on Vancouver Island, he began to realize he just didn't have the right stuff for fly fishing for speckled trout, whom he called his 'brides', and began to favour salt water, jigging for ling cod, rockfish and flounder, and unintentionally, at times hooking a heavy-bodied lunker of a wild salmon. Both freshwater and saltwater angling provided the poet with a bountiful yield of piscatorial poems.

Finally his poetic inspiration drifted inland to the Qualicum Beach Heritage Forest, where he was smitten by giant cedars, some going back centuries. Rosenblatt took copious notes of those tall trees, and being a visual artist as well as a poet, sketched them.

Although an intense cynic and not at all inclined to go the pathway of any organized mainstream religion, he gradually came to the realization that those ancient trees had souls, as did the surrounding wildlife, from frenzied woodpeckers to lowly caterpillars and centipedes. The born-again animist in Rosenblatt has come to honour the spirit of the forest in sonnets that focus on his beloved friend, the mythic Green Man, viewing these poems in praise of this arboreal deity as 'forest devotionals'. Indeed they posit the question: Is the Green Man Rosenblatt's alter ego, or is the poet, at the very least, his understudy? What to make of Rosenblatt's Green Muse?

When queried by another poet back in the nineties as to why he didn't write sensible poems about the women who adored him, he replied, 'Well, I always thought that Mother Nature was far sexier.'

Mycelium Motels

A sapling from a soggy bed is nourished by decay.
Mouldering into soil, that tree trunk is with child!
Living or dead, mothers are providers in many guises.
At a distance I hear the tapping of a beak striking a tree:
This is no cryptic code, but a woodpecker mining for bugs.
As mist from the forest floor rises to clothe me in fog apparel,
I hear my clever diner gustily extract another motherlode of grub.
Morning dew glistens on a spider's web hanging from a leaf.

But where's that sprightly engineer gone who built this gluey net?
Spores travel invisibly nearby to check in to mycelium motels.
Fretfully, a small white butterfly comes to rest on a toadstool
and there with wings aflutter it semaphores a prayer to me.
Pale little pilgrim, you've mistaken me for your celestial Maker.
Sunlight, trickle in, illume my mind's darkness and its forest.

A Paris Kitchen

A pheasant came into view, the Green Man blinked at royalty.
That ring-necked bird shook his dappled wings of many hues
and gazed with disbelief at a monarch so shabbily dressed.
No haute couturier would touch those unsightly brambles:
How does one deal with militant centipedes and millipedes?
Those mouldy leaves say a sartorial makeover isn't possible.
Transfixed, the Beau Brummell of the woods waltzed about.
He appeared to have fallen in love with his decorous plumage.

'Now who's better dressed than me?' the fop's outfit cried.
Yet there was some troubled locomotion in the dandy's stride.
His pride didn't move in sync with the hubris of his plumage!
Behind a dainty red mask a distraught psyche is concealed:
As a high-end fashion model he'd be banned from any catwalk.
But he'd be embraced in a Paris kitchen of a three-star eatery.

A Naked Waving Hand

There are lost shadows in the woods stalking other shades.
Some fading silhouette is moving in among these spooks.
A grim notion flew through my mind: This outline, is it me?
I perceive sclerotic limbs, pallid leaves and fallen branches.
Sunlight had seeped away as though absorbed into a blotter.
Gone, and yet for me, somehow, it didn't seem to matter.
A chill crept down my spine; I'd been here, but in a dream.
It was too bewildering; some apparitions had familiar faces.

Dare I ask the Green Man if he, too, could become a ghost?
To ask such a frightful question would be a grave offence:
It'd be much safer to grope the ectoplasm of a commoner.
Or have an eagle from a great height measure you for lunch.
Not every monarch can endure to be imprisoned in a tree.
Nor can an ungloved regent regrow a naked waving hand.

Choristers

A tiny jester takes a nap among sowbugs and centipedes.
The salamander is snug inside the boudoir of a rotting log.
And a silence there adheres to the filaments of dreams.
Craving the dampness of a mossy bed she lies fast asleep.
Her drab grey outfit is unappealing, best suited for a bog.
The couturier who designed that apparel had to be a fool.
Where's one to find tree frogs to make a fashionista proud?
Those baritones never sang to him: the Green Man is tearful.

A *lèse-majesté* to sylvan royalty is not redeemable on earth.
As an offence to him, you need to chant your praise aloud.
He desires some melodic company, a vocalist or two....
Can any regent of the woods be denied a burst of adulation?
Listen, crooners: Make your presence known, come into view!
My master requests a command performance of you choristers.

They've Eaten All the Leaves

Inside a silken chrysalis of a dream I heard a granulating cry.
But it was my voice I heard which echoed in the darkness.
That disquieting plea for help portended my disintegration.
'It's all spun lies, chicanery; I'll live for all eternity,' I cried.
'In my sleep I see sticky webs for me to adhere to immortality.'
And then I saw the Green Man stir inside a hollow of a tree:
'You must keep on dreaming,' his verdant eminence replied.
He was not amused; nibbling caterpillars had crept into his den.

The pilgrims had come to nest on His Majesty's floriated head.
They wished to metamorphose into swarms of sexy butterflies.
His mouth agape soon filled to capacity with gold-hued gliders.
I was prattling to myself long after my shadow had gone to bed.
As in a theatre when the lights dim, so fall the curtains of eternity.
'And where will it end,' I said, 'when they've eaten all the leaves?'

The Gruesome Self

On its tiny feet the millipede of time dawdles by.
Wafting aimlessly that cumulus could be a ghost!
I could be some somnambulating cloud in the sky.
And in the wink of a millisecond I could disappear.
His brain is wired to a chronograph in hyperspace.
The sovereign of the woods needs no fancy Rolex.
A millennium to him is but a sniffle in the ether.
Like rock and roll the Green Man will never die.

Unlike His verdant Majesty I can't regrow a limb.
Nor can I reclaim the exterior of a youthful face.
The white thatch on my pate is an eviction notice.
Gazing at the mirror I ask: Now am I out of focus?
Even in a funhouse a distorted reflection never lies.
Behind that bending glass the gruesome self dwells.

A Noiseless Meal

The darkness crept in to meet the light sidling out.
I was alone with my shadow as a sole companion.
The silence seemed a balm for a tired moth in flight.
And then I became aware of this minuscule sound:
From under a pile of leaves came a pleading voice.
It struggled to escape from that composting mound
to join the eerie morning mist rising in the woods.
Could those rags of ectoplasm be our future spooks?

Secured to a beard of moss hanging from a branch
I'm glued to a masterpiece of a spider's dewy web.
What a marvel that little engineer has nimbly spun.
Yet being nibbled by him is more a dazzling sight.
I'd rather be an emanation of a rattling poltergeist.
A glutton on the run enjoys a noiseless meal on a wire.

A Lullaby

Having no bony branches I'll never be a Sitka spruce.
Those spindly extensions are the tired fingers of a tree.
On parade, inch by inch, a thousand years shall pass.
Haunting reflections of the past drift by in single file
like a snail on the ground the feet of time move on.
And in my grandeur I'll feel I've not aged or decayed.
Asleep, I seem wide awake, and yet I've not awoken.
It's worse for the dreamer with a mouth wide open.

The Green Man spews out a red-backed salamander.
And for a superb masterpiece in decorous gastronomy:
He has a beard of climbing ivy to share with a visitor.
Luna moths blur their spectral wings in the moonlight.
They keep him wide awake by their vibratory anthem.
It's a lullaby for souls in transit to a dusky underworld.

An Infant Mewl

That ancient cedar is wearing the firmament for a hat.
A drifting cloud has come to take a nap above his head.
Now it could be just a dream—I'd say a puff of fantasy?
This dapper sentinel is holding up an eggshell-blue ceiling.
In my sleep I could pupate and change into a caterpillar.
For as each scene mutates I can't escape this feeling:
I'm some drifting dreamer unmoored in my brain....
I think the vault of heaven is full of counterfeit currency.

'Peek-a-boo,' someone whispered to a hidden child in me.
And so I thought that my noggin was haunted by a spook.
The darkness from within had welcomed a spectral lunacy.
It seemed that all creation cried, yet there was no sound.
As the Green Man shut his eyelids, I in terror lay awake
to hear an infant mewl from deep inside a foggy grove.

My Face

A rustling in the woods and then this murmur followed.
My heart and his were racing, blood and sap turned cold.
We were tied to a fear that formed into seismic follicles.
An angry axeman was about, and he was keen to get us.
I heard a splintering sound nearby: his labour had begun!
A shrill of rising laughter seemed to follow every chop.
This crazed fellow seemed more than suited for the job.
Gustily, he cachinnated with every branch he chopped.

Mayhem to him was recreational, a way of having fun.
That berserker's laughter arose to chill our ears….
And then I began to wonder if he'd been born to kill.
Did he have a nurturing mother, and did it really matter?
The Green Man wore my face while I put on his visage.
We each had donned a death mask, yet we were still alive.

Nibbled Digitals

It was a familiar utterance, as from a previous visit
when again an eerie voice crept deep into my mind.
Petrified, the surrounding leaves began to etiolate.
A limb began to bend; my head was being haunted.
I couldn't make a sound, nor could my foliated friend.
Gloomily, we shared a hideaway in some shady grove
where ectoplasmic moss climbed to cover up our faces.
And caterpillars arrived to hide us beneath a foamy tent.

Time is a ravenous monster—no end to his devouring.
He has a ferocious appetite and stomachs to be filled.
The beast is no respecter of paupers or verdant royalty.
Everything seems digestible with this dark gastronome.
The diner would view his intestinal tract as an appetizer.
If he could find his nibbled digitals, they'd be finger food.

Osmosis

Adorned in leaves and brambles, we're quite a sight to see
as neck to neck, the Green Man and I reside inside a tree.
One couldn't ask for finer company than this camaraderie.
Time seemed at rest in the arms of elongated branches
where shadows desire to commingle with other apparitions.
It was there I sought to find the Stygian darkness in myself.
I saw His Majesty shed a tear, and thought it very strange.
How could any noblesse in wood display such affection?

But it wasn't me that he wept for, but for himself alone.
He was royalty, and I, a commoner, was still dismayed.
Yet we shared a plate and nibbled on sadness and despair.
The meat of grief I find is edible, despite some gristle—
and we topped off our dining with crème de chlorophyll.
I sipped my drink normally and he tasted his by osmosis.

An Invasive Alien

In fondling trees, I confess to brazen acts of intimacy.
Yet in touching them I locate that sylvan part of me.
A hand desires to become a limb sprouting leaves.
There's so much amorosity in stroking a lower branch:
Silently, those giants stand as glum immobile sentinels.
The tallest cedar in the group wears an eagle for a hat.
As my feet move underground they mutate into roots.
They greedily absorb moisture, nutrients, and minerals.

The soul can become a hydrated sponge for a drinker.
Yet I need the water to quench the thirst of every leaf.
I trust the other cedar won't see me as an invasive alien.
It doesn't really matter; for them, I'll always be a stranger.
Nor shall I don a matching raptor for some fancy headgear.
My skin is turning into bark—my heart is filled with fear.

Sharing His Prickly Crown of Thorns

In the silence of his lair the Green Man grew another eye.
A needy red-breasted sapsucker mistook it for some grub.
Hunger has a stomach all its own, and a matching snout.
That famished fellow in his frenzy, pecked it cleanly out
and the other eye—it, too, could be mistaken for a bug!
Any drumming beak fills His verdant Majesty with fear.
Yet a warbler's distant song can delight any human ear.
This bird once sang on a limb protruding from a lofty head.

To my surprise, as in some crowded asphyxiating dream
I became attached to my unsmiling master of the woods.
It seemed I couldn't free myself from that super mucilage.
The viridescent potentate and I were conjoined at the hip.
Stems of leaves and dappled fungi sprouted from our nostrils.
Yet I felt privileged in sharing his prickly crown of thorns.

His Majesty Is Waiting

A frantic spider strides across a window of my mind.
He's there to feed on my thoughts adhering to his net.
Waltzing in the air, he exudes a gluey silver filament.
Sometimes that traveller comes to rest above my brow.
Refreshed after a micro nap, this spinner is unglued.
Rappelling down on a thread to meet me eye to eye....
Awed by his octagonal artistry and frozen by his gaze—
those gelid eyes were telling me I was staring at myself.

I'm touched by an unyielding sadness in these woods.
Gazing at a passerby, each tree wears a pensive face.
A midday shadow of a butterfly lies resting on a stump.
Its gloomy wings semaphore a message out to me:
His Majesty is waiting to receive you ... don't be late.
Peer down at your likeness beneath his floriated mask.

Mining for Bugs

Who let the darkness through the cat door of my brain?
As well, this tentacle of a branch came rustling through
to make itself cozily at home deep in my upper storey.
I was all alone, and much afraid of that ghostly limb.
It spooked me as it spiralled and wriggled in a waltz.
Like vipers inside a jar, my mind serves as a vessel
where my muse stirs, riven with undulating thoughts.
Spitting out a caterpillar, the Green Man, too, is haunted.

And then out of his mouth pops a second fuzzy visitor.
As a gurgling sinkhole would go on swallowing a lake
I want to see my gloom disappear down a thirsty drain.
His Majesty is in terror of some nearby drumming sound.
A woodpecker's frenzied tapping takes his breath away.
Any hungry bird, mining for bugs, can bore into an eyeball.

Motes of Night

Their eyes suddenly appear each time I paint a tree.
They have a chilly look as they gaze defiantly at me
yet I'm beaming back at them to bend their hostility.
In this joust of willpower, there's no quarter given:
For it's a frightful war, by way of ophthalmic voltage.
I'll confess to having surrendered to arboreal beauty.
In gawking at a multi-eyed giant, my sap always freezes.
Spooked, I turn my face away from that towering cedar.

The Green Man's many underlings are on surveillance.
I'm eyeballed everywhere I go in these haunted woods.
When motes of night shadow me, and I am all alone
I crave for sparkling fireflies to illumine the darkness.
As a moth charging at a flame I'd brush aside the evening.
But I'd never dash inside the hollow of his royal chamber.

The Entrance

Supposing these decaying stumps of tree could talk.
What would they say to me, a stranger, passing by?
That they don't seem to mind, sustaining the living
as they turn into soil, and provide food for a sapling.
And the dead absorb water to quench a toddler's thirst.
Some greenness is wholesome for that growing child.
My fading body is in need of a healthier complexion.
I appear too pale—my skin doesn't seem quite natural.

On tiny feet, the sublime, shuffles beneath a forest floor
to hear an intriguing melody in the trickling of a stream.
The Green Man's soul has been there for a vitalizing bath.
I believe it's my turn, but I have yet to find the entrance.
And if I find that secret portal, there are dangers to be faced
such as a vigorous laving in the bathhouse of a termitarium.

His Majesty Is Afraid

Wanting to find memory's earth-scented truffle
deep, deep into that black soil of darkness I dug
and sniffed those fragrances most precious to me.
Nostalgia has a gifted snout, and a kissable mouth:
Reminiscences are savoured, smooched, and devoured.
The Green Man has been steadily bitten, he knows
that my existence, and his, is a chewable experience
where Lady Fate set up her groaning board of edibles.

And I've seen the sun appear as a fiery dinner plate.
In one's life, a bit of nibbling is not a terrible thing.
There are stirrings under a pile of composting leaves.
My nerves have scurried beneath that mound to hide.
His Majesty is afraid—tent caterpillars have arrived!
They've come to set up camp and feed above his face.

Gilding the Sadness

In delight the Green Man's eyes shone and dilated
as they beheld a playful sight of moving caterpillars
who drifted slowly in single file as in a fuzzy dream.
It was a view to tingle every ringlet of his leafy beard.
At heart he was a sentimentalist of the weeping kind.
Once he cried in witnessing a moth spiral to its death.
He saw it trembling on the ground in the lunar light.
And he wept when its wings semaphored goodbye.

I must gather up some sunshine and refine it into gold
and pour that glowy soup, drip by drip, into my brain
gilding the sadness inside and setting my mind aglow.
There's rustling deep inside the throne room of a tree.
His Majesty is looking pale and a bit dispirited today.
He's one in need of an elixir to waft those blues away.

Greener

There are many haunting spirits in these silent woods.
I feel their presence as I wander along a winding trail.
Hearing the sound of splintered wood in a falling tree
I'm made aware that a beginning is ligatured to an end.
A garter snake sloughs off its skin to grow another hide.
In envy, I dare to ask: *Why don't I have that kind of magic?*
I'd gladly become his shadow undulating in the daylight
and shimmy on the ground beneath some ghostly moss.

Moving like a millipede the darkness nibbles on a soul.
There's nowhere for me—time itself faces devourment
for as I'm being nibbled, there'll be nothing left to view.
Under the Green Man's foliated face a grim visage is hidden
that bears a frightful resemblance to the maker of this sonnet.
I'll need to let some sunlight in to make my psyche greener.

A Painted Lady

A voice moved into my noggin and crept inside my brain.
It caught me by surprise: *Are you sketching me?* it hissed.
I was scorned by a sibilating cedar, something was amiss.
Or was this plaintive cry conveyed from my soul to me?
Yet, it seemed I knew the very source of that eerie whisper.
'So you want to grow as tall as me,' it said, and prattled on:
'You're not the one to be my understudy, if that's your wish.'
The Green Man was not amused by my emboldened musing.

Adding hurt to insult, I had sketched the anger in his eyes.
Yet he seemed gratified in knowing I couldn't grow a limb.
I was bereft of greenery, having neither leaves nor branches.
Not every woodland pilgrim wants to be a prodigious tree.
Now a birder might ogle some chestnut-backed chickadee
while the lepidopterist flutters at the sight of a painted lady.

The Motility of a Millipede

In lieu of a rabbit, I've pulled the darkness out of a hat
and set the dimness beside a glow of forest greenery.
Out spilled shards of cerulean blue from a cruising sky.
The Green Man took no notice of my act, he fell asleep.
Yet, when I hauled out a sapling, he suddenly awoke
and spewed up some moss, while his lips formed a smile.
I surmised that he had recognized a sprouting grandchild.
His eyes glistened with pride—I thought he would weep.

I say it'd be quite a trick to pull the daylight out of a hat.
Yet a grander show would be to retrieve all of eternity
to spread it as a sparkling blanket over a plump rabbit.
And when in bed, I'd settle for the night as my comforter.
The Green Man views infinity in the motility of a millipede.
Yet I can only see those slow minuscule legs of the present.

If One Regenerates a Limb

Red-backed salamanders scuttle beneath a rotting log
to nibble a trail through a world of moistened darkness.
They all take refuge and nestle in that dimness of my fear
and I'll not let the sunlight in to despoil the pristine night.
There's seepage in my mind, luminescence is leaking in.
Metamorphosed, I've become a jittery four-legged spirit.
I'll eat every granule of light that'll fit into my mouth.
Above me, I feel a seismic quaver of a predacious snout.

Fate moves across the forest floor sniffing for a meal.
Wafted by a breeze, a prey exudes a discernible aroma.
As salamanders and their incarnations dash and hide
I ponder what morsels of my being would taste like.
Such gustatory dining in the woods is purely fanciful.
But such gustation is possible, if one can sacrifice a limb.

An Obesity of Gloom

The Green Man lost a limb yet it didn't seem to bother him.
For he could regrow another branch to replace the one he lost.
He faced his share of mutilations from impious tree carvers.
But what he feared most was the spray from some pit bull
as urine from that beast seeped inside to profane his soul.
A thug once initialed his name below his royal residence.
He hemorrhaged sap at the sight of that awful desecration
while on his face, a swaddle of leaves faded and expired.

The woods have eyes to see that any wounded tree bleeds.
And when those mourners wail—it's not the wind one hears.
The Green Man's mouth is filled with snuggly caterpillars.
His cry is muffled and his doleful eyes are awash in tears.
Soon he and all the forest sway in their familial grieving.
Unable to contain an obesity of gloom, a puffball bursts.

Growl

'Don't despair,' the sunlight whispered to the night.
The darkness then replied, 'I must be quite a fright.'
Luminescence was in retreat, no reply was ever sent.
As I lie hidden in the roots of the past and the present
my sombre thoughts are eaten by multitudes in green.
Every tree seems awake in the silence of these woods.
Yet I feel I'm still asleep, or sleepwalking in a dream.
Aged bones and flesh mutate into leaves and branches.

Malformed as a hybrid, he has a kindly human face.
Did he have a dad, and I wonder who his mother was?
I implore the Green Man to move some crooked limb.
Yes, I see your raging eyes and that distorted mouth.
Show me you're still alive, stir a leaf or two, and growl.
He'll live forever installed inside the hollow of a tree.

Kisses

Trees touching other trees invoke goings-on of romance.
For arboreal propinquity implies a sex life in these woods.
I fear the claustrophobic intimacy in a stand of giant cedar;
What happens at evening in the forest must be frightful:
Imagine the sound of rutting branches and cruising roots?
Hear the rustling of leaves and the whispers lovers make.
And where's the Green Man in this flux of woodland eros?
Does he sense the intensity and surge of sylvan ardour?

His bones are twigs and branches and he wears a leafy mask.
Yet should his seekers find him they'll strip away the leaves.
As thieves they're bound to steal that luminosity in his eyes.
And a few have found his lips and profaned them with a kiss!
As his tongue resists their kisses he's left with a bitter aftertaste.
He'd much prefer to have his lips pressed by a maternal ghost.

The Loving Mom He Never Knew

A restive shadow followed me no bigger than an ant.
It softly pressed against my heels in its haste to pass.
I then began to think my quest was coming to an end.
Yet I didn't care where the trail ended in these woods.
Some follicle of a passing apparition was off its leash.
It shimmered on the ground as it trekked along with me.
Or was that bit of shade a thread, a filigree of memory?
The past is a filament that is famished for the present.

There's a grove in the forest where I can be at peace
to reflect upon some sapling, a newborn on a nurse log.
Once a child, the Green Man, too, had a selfless mother.
As a seedling of an orphan, he grew in his momma's soil.
Branches swish and crackle and a teardrop falls on a leaf.
I believe he's thinking of the loving mom he never knew.

Outing Him

A pensive face appears inside a black onyx bowl
as croutons in my brain float above a fungal broth.
Yet there's no one about to share this soup, but me.
I shall invite some slug to bathe in that soup du jour.
He'll serve as a condiment to flavour my concoction.
There'll be no other additives to enhance that chowder.
For this is a grotty gumbo for only me alone to taste.
Yet a bit of salt would accentuate this murky repast.

Drawing his nutrients deeply from beneath the ground
the reflective Green Man prefers to dine alone …
for one can be a gourmand and still live inside a tree.
Fluffy snuffling poodles have been close to outing him
peeing at the base of his dwelling as a mark of respect.
Yet they'll not sniff him out and I won't reveal his lair.

Alabaster Moons

Smothered under an embroidery of leaves and branches
I saw an outline of his face in my dream, in chiaroscuro.
It seemed I had become the Green Man's confidant.
And yet I feared the enclosing darkness of the forest.
There was no place to hide for me and my timid shadow.
I was a few steps ahead of my umbrageous companion
but in our haste we were followed by incandescent spooks.
Their luciferin flashed an urgent ghostly light in the night.

I want to neatly fold the evening in two as I would a napkin
or squeeze the stomach of a nocturnal sky to liberate its ink.
There's a stash to be had if I could open the vault of heaven:
One by one I'd place those stars into a bottomless velvet bag
and shamelessly I'd snatch a multitude of alabaster moons
to string a pearl necklace and tempt the Green Man's mistress.

A Mossy Gruel

A muffled cry is heard deep inside a big leaf maple grove.
There the Green Man attempts to articulate a plea for help.
It's all in vain, he's choking, words slide down his throat!
How can he speak when his mouth is full of soggy moss?
An addled mind wanders freely to hide among some ferns
as in my brain, green mingles with umber brown and grey.
In that funereal silence I find I'm really talking to a sapling.
And this lonely tyke is an orphan sprouting on a decaying log.

Upon exiting its body, the self becomes a wandering snail.
I've viewed that little pilgrim inching along the forest floor.
I surmise it's on a scent trail and won't be coming home.
It could be I've written my obituary or a dirge to my soul.
A growl thunders through the woods, followed by a roar.
Branches snap and then I know he's expelled a mossy gruel.

The Wild Man

His grey-blue eyes appeared to clash with his pallid lips.
I've tried to get his leaf-strewn face to converse with me.
I believe he's learned to sleep with his eyes wide open.
He blinked when I promised him to keep his den a secret.
Knowing I could keep a promise, a smile formed on his lips.
It didn't matter whether he was asleep, or in another state—
the centuries have passed and still he hasn't said a word!
Yet his breathing has caused those etiolated leaves to stir.

In my craving to be that green hopeful to the Green Man
I'll don a verdant costume and perform a shamanic dance—
pay homage to his Eminence entombed inside a cedar tree.
The spirit of the Wild Man demands respect and veneration.
Psyches flutter here and there, or wither on a woodland vine
and memories are covered up in a mound of spongy moss.

I Want

I heard a mocking laughter from somewhere in the woods
and sensed this cachinnation gusted from a foliated head.
It was a leafy noggin that I'd seen in a cinematic dream.
The lord protector of these woods is a boisterous fellow.
Yet he'll shed his lustre like a snake sloughing off its skin—
for when I saw him last his face had a lesser tint of green.
He was losing chlorophyll and a bit of paleness had set in.
Yet under his leafy mask that feral man kept on glowing.

His spirit is indomitable—and he won't let it go astray.
I want to be a greener man than he who rules this forest.
How can I wrest the power from that unsmiling potentate?
A voice in my belfry desires that I be interred inside a tree.
I'll not abide the creepy moss moving in and choking me.
The driving rain turns the soul to rot and that is terrifying.

Chipping Away

On a nurse log children grow among some sword ferns.
Even from the netherworld a mother's job is never done.
Her spirit sustains her brood near that decomposing log.
A cumulus of tears envelops me as from another realm.
She's lingering in the fog rising from the forest floor.
I see apparitions in mounds of climbing feather mosses.
They'll serve as a spongy reservoir for a thirsty stump.
The perfect mom sends her ectoplasmic love in the mist.

I see a raven ascend to a branch and hear his soliloquy.
Or it's a panegyric from a gourmand cloaked all in black.
An egg abandoned in a nest will do for a zesty appetizer.
If he's in luck he's bound to spot a passing soul in flight.
The Green Man has seen this spectacle acted out before.
Chipping away at his prey the bird has you and me in mind.

A Toy

Passing by a decorously leafy head jutting out of a tree
I countenanced a grim visage adorned in a vibrant green.
It matched the blue of my eyes and proved a visual delight.
I'm in no mood for company someone hoarsely whispered.
At first I thought I'd undergone an auditory hallucination.
But what I heard was the voice of a reigning sovereign.
A patch of sunlight shone upon the greenness of his face.
The Green Man frowned as branches on his hands stirred.

He was none too pleased to view an invasive commoner.
I intuited by his gaze that I was ranked below a termite.
A chartreuse-yellow tongue flared out from his mouth.
And yet I discerned gentility in him as his anger piqued
while all around me the evening hissed like a feral cat.
The darkness surrounded me and played me like a toy.

Oblivion

This well-trod pathway in the woods leads to a rustic pub.
A deep-green-hued patron there hoists a mug of amber ale.
Often he's joined by a roustabout who enjoys a pint or two.
His pal has no face and the brew they drink is never empty
for the barman has told the pair the drinks are on the house.
Yet he's too spooked to be a waiter and approach their table.
And what server wouldn't be awed by a hefty tip left behind?
There's a treasury to be fondled in millipedes and caterpillars.

My magic critters have all dissolved—that's fiction for you!
They were never there at all and neither was that watering hole.
This sylvan poet sends his soul perambulating on a narrow trail.
Will a tiny speck of his personality come fluttering back to him?
A troubled thought drags a thousand tiny feet along the ground
to follow a brigade of ants fleeing under a stump to Oblivion.

A Momma's Boy

Not an easy one to find, although he's staring out at you.
At times I thought I'd seen a shimmering in his eyes.
And I've sensed a gnarled fury embedded in his nature
as though his amiability had been devoured by fire ants.
A pleading voice trickled out from a thicket in the forest:
Look beneath the tallest cedar dwarfing those other trees.
He's concealed, but you'll find him starved for company.
A sapling I couldn't see was compelled to talk with me.

Young, old, reborn, and those departing, harbour secrets
to be shared with the likes of some sympathetic passerby?
I think the Green Man is still attached to his mother's navel.
Eight hundred years have passed and he's still a momma's boy!
There are many rural watering holes named after that overlord.
Yet you'll not find him at any pub where they welcome dogs.

An Aviator's Waltz

The hibernacula in my brain fill with frenetic thought.
They hum a mournful song to me before they hibernate.
And in their sleep they urge to be awoken in the spring.
In these woods one is aroused, or continues sleeping.
A playful red admiral butterfly alights upon my shoulder.
By his wings' articulation I think he wants to have a chat.
He gyrates above my head to perform an aviator's waltz.
Is he signalling for a partner to share his short waltzing life?

He has eaten up the light and left not a bit of glow for me.
I'm too entombed in my head to leave and talk with him.
Why would I talk with anyone who dwells inside a tree?
The darkness has soiled all the sunny spaces in the forest.
My thoughts flutter as they ascend toward a brighter sky—
for each reflection needs to warm its wings in the sunlight.

Viewing a Midday Lunch

A Stygian black ghost slithers from under a mound of leaves.
I see a line of green scribed along his side as he passes me.
In fright, I step back from that Beau Brummell of a reptile.
His body lengthens to send the friendliest of signals to me.
And I exclaim: 'You've awoken far too early from your nap.'
He glares at me as though I'm trespassing on his grand estate.
'What have you caught today?' I ask this longitudinal dandy.
Yet I envision his menu: Slugs, baby birds, worms and mice.

In these woods even dreams are eaten by a slim garter snake.
I and the Green Man know: *Life makes a meal of the living.*
And still he hides, dreading to be a scratchpad for some cougar.
From the perch on a treetop a bald eagle eyes a catch of the day.
Might I not appear as a mouse to a raptor viewing a midday lunch?
Like a snail, I hurry away carrying a house on my crooked back.

Betrayed

A Lady of the woods wears a veil of leaves to hide her tears.
For by her side stands her faithless consort, the Green Man.
He bears a shameful face beneath a mask of etiolated leaves.
Has he no conscience, his heart, is it made of gnarled wood?
And I think of each uncared-for orphan sapling left all alone.
They're still in need of nourishment and parental guidance.
Extend a leafy branch—they're starved for a parental hug.
Cease your sneaking off to your strumpet for a romantic fix.

His mistress is a neighbour living in an adjoining cedar.
A sylvan beauty, she's too immature in adoring older men.
In cellulose or flesh, they arrive to snuggle in the forest.
There's simply no stopping them when their sap goes wild.
My weary soul goes shuffling off on a hundred tired feet
as that howling mother of the woods is again betrayed.

His Meditation

A red-backed salamander slinked across a soggy log.
Seeking to be left alone it sped into a world of decay.
A critter costumed in red, yellow, green and black.
What couturier dared to dream up such an outfit?
And as it vanished I saw salt and pepper on its belly.
Yet that slim wanderer was better dressed than me.
Was I predestined to judge some brightly hued fop?
This lizard was a winner, even if the colours clashed!

The polychromatic poet has both feet on the ground.
His thoughts move like a millipede as he cogitates:
The soul, he wonders—can it possess a thousand feet?
And from a great height a hungry eagle is viewing him.
It would appear they can read this frightened little man.
Moss climbs up his legs as his meditation disintegrates.

Famished

Lonely as a gastropod dragging its house on the ground
the Green Man lacks a loving spouse to share his life.
No greenish lady has he to trim his crowded leafy beard.
Morbidly shy, he's always hiding, how can he find a wife?
The silent type, he prefers to play his game of invisibility:
He's afraid of meeting up with the beak of a woodpecker.
Yet more fearful is the wheeze of that woodsman's snout.
As a gifted organ it can detect subatomic particles of fear.

An axe can serve as a nose aligned to the wedge of a face.
That edge is the creative side of a berserker's personality!
The woods can see who's waiting at the end of every trail.
What pathway do I take to escape that grinning lunatic?
I see him dragging a rucksack over his sloping shoulders.
Perhaps he's famished for a patch of golden chanterelles?

The Markings of a Soul

Like pale arrivals from a doughy planet devoid of sunlight
an extended family of oyster mushrooms appear on a log.
Seeming sad, and yet they're a shade happier than me.
Spores of immortality convene upon a wet forest floor.
They're invisible, yet I see appearances of newborn fungi:
In their tumescence they convey an excess of felicity.
My alien friends, I see the future in a decaying tree trunk.
Sprouting voyeurs are in bloom looking here and there.

And in their flourishing can we say there's no beginning
nor an end, just continuance, look, the Green Man grins:
He can't speak, there's far too much moss in his mouth.
The markings of a soul are on the wings of a magpie moth.
Chasing a shadow it bolts into the darkness and I wonder—
my reflections, are they fed inside this gloomy sonnet?

The Solitude

I deny I'm the current owner of a face masked in foliage.
I'd much prefer to see my real mug on an all-points bulletin.
Who hides beneath that leafage and protruding branches?
Sought out by talent scouts you could become hot property.
I see you showcased with the bearded lady in a freak show.
Am I to assume that you're ashamed of being different?
Tear away those crazy leaves, and reveal your true kisser:
I'm sure there are others like you in some heritage forest.

Don't be afraid, I won't give your hiding place away.
Let me help unburden you of your decorous vegetation:
Now why do you gaze at me with those woeful eyes?
I only wish to be a friend and share the solitude with you.
A worried godhead resides under all that tangled greenery
who dreams he's becoming a dartboard in a country pub.

My Indwelling

Reflecting upon a nurse log I envy each sprouting child
issuing from a parental soil of composting bark on a stump.
It would seem a mother's longing for her children never ends.
Orphaned before they were born, they never knew their mom.
Yet I sense a maternal spirit in each drop of rain on a sapling.
I hear the brittle branches bend and snap in the eerie silence.
No sentimentalist, that jubilating woodsman, his fetish, an axe!
I don't believe he ever had a happy childhood, or a loving dad.

But why should he care—the terminator loves decaying matter.
The woods have tiny eyes to view some passing tree molester.
They see through the leafage of my doubts, denials and desires.
A self-proclaimed green monk in the cathedral of a forest muses:
If they could speak, they'd cry: *Touch me, touch me everywhere.*
My indwelling, I say to you: *Show your love, go and hug a tree!*

Enter the Darkness

Sometimes on a nature trail one needs a faithful companion.
Like a dog on a leash, or the fond remembrance of a lover.
I enter the darkness of the woods and embrace the silence.
An endearing friend and protector, the solitude follows me.
Some forest sparrows soar high above the rooftop of my mind.
I hear the crunch of his axe and the sound of splintered wood.
And I'm fearful of the stranger who's not your blissful pilgrim.
The stranger wears the evening for a face, stars for his eyes.

He does a graceful bow when passing a newborn sapling.
Giddier than a red-breasted sapsucker chipping away at a bug
that hooded forester dons a smile with each rhapsodic chop!
Behind swathes of leaves, branches and brambles, I've hidden.
His illuminating eyes light up my brow as they search for me.
My blood commingles with the sap trickling deep inside a tree.

Camouflage

I have a rendezvous to keep with the Green Man's Lady.
She's a clothing aficionado, all garbed in climbing lichen.
And I mustn't keep her waiting by that old nurse log.
Overdressed, frightened, suspicious of every passerby:
Tree groper and birder, they'll never know she's there.
Yet I alone discern a glare emanating from her teary eyes.
A cold bioluminescent light pulses in the darkened forest.
And my brain is set aglow to sparkle as by divine ignition.

The iridescence of her silvery eyebrows stirs at my approach
while her lips of opalescent green pout to form a shapely kiss.
Why hide such a resplendent body under so much foliage?
I want to slip beneath those leaves and be with her at rest.
And let my hands run wild over her naked thighs and bosom:
I'm in camouflage, my dear, search beneath my skin for me.

The Rapture

Capillarity has raised the libido up from the roots to their lips.
In a dank room of the Hotel Osmosis the Green Man caresses
a vamp of a tree, leafless, she's pregnant with everlasting life.
Deciduous, she's still the looker wafting an earthy truffle scent
while her itchy paramour extends his humid roots out to hers.
On an unmade bed they lie grasping at each other's branches.
They're unaware there's a voyeur wanting in on the action.
The pair is being ogled by some Fancy Dan of a chanterelle.

Here's an unflappable roué in pursuit of his bountiful pleasure.
He's scented in earthy fragrances to match a golden radiance.
The rapture in romantic junkies can turn a pigment greener
while that carnal sweetness in the flesh becomes diseased.
And I who blindly wander along a snow-filled forest path
reflect upon escaping a lunatic, his squally wrath and axe.

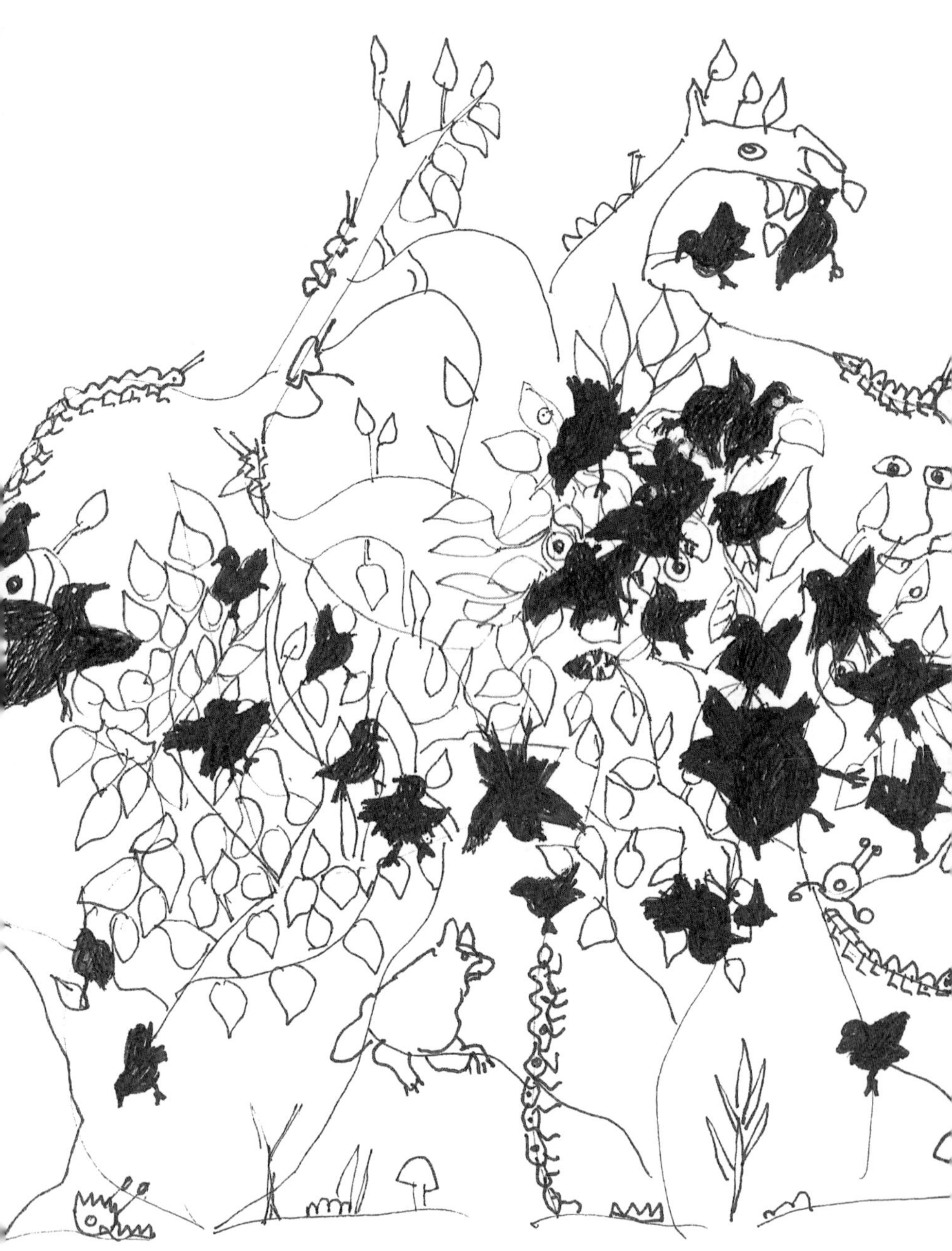

Photosynthesis Motel

Is there a suitable Green Woman for the Green Man?
Branch to leafy branch I see them joined at the hip.
Transfixed by a glow dancing in each other's eyes:
The two so deeply submerged in love's viridescence.
Theirs is a longing held together by a super mucilage.
In a darkened forest it's not unusual for lustful couples
to have a craving for conjoining or share a solar bath?
The marquee lights up on the Photosynthesis Motel.

Attired in wild fern, salal, and moss of emerald green
they're greeted by a puffball at a seedy reception desk.
'Will it be for one night or will you be staying longer?'
'We're only staying overnight,' reply his surly guests
piqued by the smiley attitude of a patronizing fungus.
'And yes, we'll need a king-size bed as we're together.'

A Lighter Shade of Green

A face is concealed in the splendour of surrounding greenery.
Leaves grow out of his nostrils, ears, mouth, and forehead
and often I've met the unfriendly gaze of his opalescent eyes;
to find myself transfixed by a profile immersed in leafage.
In these silent woods the Green Man has no fixed address.
But if I can't locate him … perhaps he can seek me out?
An aged wayfarer in an ill-fitting jacket I can easily be found.
Unsteady in my waddling, I carry a crooked walking stick.

That twisty stick takes me to where I think I ought to go.
The feral mind like a shadow drifts dreamily in a forest
past families of oyster mushrooms sleeping on a log.
I hear a rustling in nearby foliage and then a whisper
beckons me to go attired in a lighter shade of green.
'We have the tree to ourselves,' the Green Man says.

My Mug

Swept into a jubilant beard of lucent green moss
the Green Man is hiding inside the hollow of a tree.
Yet I may have passed his face smothered in foliage.
Perhaps I was projecting, or simply staring at myself?
I'm your basic rustic, that simple woodland voyeur.
His grey eyes seem familiar, and that beastly grin—
I think my mug is staring out from a decaying stump!
Am I profiled on a tree trunk to frighten passersby?

You'll find a visage such as mine in any heritage forest.
But who'd go tête-à-tête to meet my olivaceous kisser?
A lovesick warbler might chance it, and plant a kiss.
And I can see a woodpecker drilling kisses on my lips.
Less adoring is that berserker wielding his beloved axe.
He leers at me, and says: 'My friend, you need a shave!'

My Devotional

I'm drawn to a newborn in need of parental fondling.
Sprouting through decaying bark on some rotting log.
Nourished by a protective spirit caring for her child
that sapling has the appearance of a healthy toddler.
A sprig of affection comes with each budding shoot:
Particles of a mother thrive in composting vegetation.
Nearby, tribes of chanterelle meet upon a forest floor
to carry their golden light to a sombre neighbourhood.

The muse is in its stride as I craft this devotional.
You'll find me on a page leaning against a puffball:
We're quite the pair, yours truly, and the portly alien.
I keep tumescing while he appears lean and normal.
He teleports a thought: *Our warranty is running out.*
And his cogitation is followed by a derisive laughter.

Awakening

I wear a set of pointy ears to hear the whir of wings
for I'm that blurry moth fluttering into a sunlit forest
where the very stillness embraces one in need of rest.
Why is every passing shadow frightened by my shade?
I could be a clown upsetting the child in every ghost.
Inside a dream cocoon my thoughts ingest the larval self
dangling from a mossy beard on a branch of Douglas fir.
How I crave to be a scrumptious meal for a hungry bird.

Yet other dreamers, too, provide their own nourishment.
Germinating poltergeists are fed under blankets of decay.
It's a family affair as the dead go on to feed the living
and fungi go and canoodle under composting leaves:
Steamy puffballs convene in all their glory at this orgy.
Swelling in pride as they praise another Awakening.

My Thirsty Roots

I found solace inside a dream
and slept upon a bed of gossamer
spun by a frantic little traveller.
I dreamt I became an ancient cedar.
Outstretched arms held up the sky
while my thirsty roots slowly drank
the burbling water of Oblivion
trickling from some nearby brook.

The Boat

This is not just some passing fishing boat
powered by a weighty engine bubbling
testicular fumes … smoky testosterone.
There'll be three of us on-board: My soul and I
accompanied by a flask of fortifying rum.

I'll carry no lethal fishing rod to jig
for salmon, rockfish, ling cod, or flounder
whose harlequin mouths whisper a prayer
while they vacuum grub in the sediment.

I'm not an angler, just a thoughtful pilgrim.

Angelic Wings

For Ken Kirkby, landscape painter, Vancouver Island

Hello, infinite robin-blue cloudless personality.
Your face seems familiar—have we met before?
Mister Sky, you're a lake concealing troutly eyes.

There'll be no gurgling outboard engine to spook
those iridescent fish I want to catch and release.
I fancy a boat with oars for me and my soul.

I want to drift around awhile and cast
some sunny dry seductive artificial fly
keeping it afloat with its angelic wings.

Hey, I see a riffle—I'll cast in that direction
to entice a passing nibbly speckled phantom.
I think I'll tie my essence to a floating line.

I'll try a double loop and cast it out to God.
Or maybe I'll wait awhile and just keep drifting.
Ken, those speckled trout fold their fins in prayer.

Nature

She has set up a canvas on an easel
viewing Ken as a sexy alpha tree
wild and leafy with viridescent libido.
Nature can think, but can she paint?

'Say, who's the damned painter here,' he grouses.
'Lady, I want some slow-drying oil on my body.
Use your natural turpentine, bitch, thin me out.
And another thing: I want more leafage and shadow!'

Sketching

Ogling an artist completing a sketch
a steely emperor on the highest branch stirs.
Talons ready, he'll swoop down, and seize
what he's mistaken for scrumptious quarry.

And like some warrior god, he'll swiftly jet
skyward to a nest filled with fragmentary bones.
Yet Ken keeps on sketching that statuary bird
who sketches him in the carborundum silence.

Hello, Mister Lonely

The mottled rocks on the beach seem funereally silent.
'I want to put all of you in the post-volcanic picture.'
In a minutiae of exacting brushwork on a canvas
Ken paints a pebbly beach born of the Big Sneeze.

'Hello, Mister Lonely,' their metamorphic mouths whisper.
'So you're back again, I suppose, to capture our symmetry?'
He ignores those nasty stones who are trying to provoke him.
'Bring the lake over to us—we haven't had a drop in ages.'

'Patience, I'll bring the lake over in my painting,' Ken replies.
'I want to capture the sunlight spilling on you—Don't move!'

Silence Is an Animal

He is familiar with the oblong shadow
moving in the lake at mid-afternoon
and the eagle resting on the treetop—
that raptor can smell droplets of fear.

Silence is an animal speaking with Ken.
An honour to be observed by that bird
who's a prolific painter in his own right
spattering blood on a canvas of sky and earth.

Congealing Spirits

Out for a thrill, wanting to romp with sunlight
a poodle-cumulus is off its leash in the sky
adrift above a mountain lake, so placidly still
as to appear asleep in some darkened cradle
where tranquility rises up as disembodied mist.

Congealing spirits wander over to a solitary figure
onshore to visit a painting forming on canvas.
Ken, must be aware of an immeasurable loneliness
in a cloud famished for a dab of sunflower-yellow?
Solitude is a friend you take out for a casual stroll.

The Bird in the Stillness

The bird in the Stillness is waiting.
Talons ready to make a lusty kill—
feathers bristling, a song from hell
shrilling from his vibrant beak …

A furnace is aglow in his terrible eyes.
Has he mistaken me for a field mouse?
He's come for me and I'm still asleep.
Friend, I'm not ready to fly away with you.

A Conversation between a Mountain and a Lake

1.

Nibbling parsecs of tranquility, a mountain
peered at the lake wearing a blissful exterior.

2.

Said the lonely mountain: 'Hello out there.'
A coy body of voiceless blue water rippled.

3.

'Do you know who I am?' the mountain gusted.
'I'm not to be ignored, I've been watching you.'

4.

'I know you have, big boy,' cooed the lake.
'I like the dark silent type, head in the clouds.'

5.

'Come on down,' she whispered to her suitor
her breathy voice, so silken, it was barely audible.

6.

'I shall drink every drop of you,' he sibilated
while his shoulders shivered in their dominance.

7.

'I like a hunk with an insatiable hunger,' she purred.
'You do?' he gasped, unnerved by her lewdness.

8.

He yearned to cradle her darkly in his arms
as lovers do when broiled in senseless heat.

9.

Their romance seemed geomorphic in its intensity
yet bound to cool like volcanic plasma lapping water.

10.

Entombed inside a glaciated despair, his voice granulated.
'I see fish drowning in your depths,' he squalled, in envy.

11.

She moved silently like some ravenous trout
pursuing an undulant minnow, for a midday snack.

12.

A penumbra of jealousy slowly enshrouded him.
'You're seeing someone else; say it isn't true!'

13.

Moved by the rhythm of her breath, aqueous in its guile
a shadow shimmied across the meniscus to taunt him.

14.

Pity him who turns a crooked spine away from Beauty
repressing an embedded appetite of irrepressible urges.

15.

Too late, too late, betrayal was in the pale blue air.
She's fled with a servile company of dappled lovers.

16.

On a bed adorned in a raiment of agglutinated lip to dewy lip
she's theirs for an endless foreplay of a love that has no name.

17.

His muted rage roiled and entwined itself in ectoplasm
each time she offered her flashing thighs to a stranger.

18.

Glancing at her mountain who wore a broody cloud,
'I have my needs,' came her cry lofting to his roost.

19.

The day wore a long doleful face veiled in tearful droplets.
'I see a rainshadow. I do believe it'll pour,' said the painter.

Old Age Is a Tree with Decaying Bark

Shadows are lurking in the daylight.
Tentacles of my being stir and touch
mottled spirits congealed in a wound.
Old age is a tree with decaying bark
where voices trapped in cellulose
rage at sprouting rootlets in the earth.
Among unseen spores adrift in mildewed air
I'd be reborn, nourished by the forest floor:
I could become a child to some spongy mother.
A hawk-eyed Horus awaits us in these woods.
This bird of the Highest Order is in his roost.
He's there to snatch my soul and skyward bolt.
Shadows are lurking in the daylight.
Elfin spirits stir under decaying leaves.
We serve as food for famished fungi.
Or I could be mould on a crooked branch
where woodpeckers drumming for grubs
lay frantic claim to the same living tree.
Yellow-tailed warblers gossip by a brook
where spores of drifting memory desire
oyster mushrooms on a soggy tree trunk.

Shadows in the Woods

You, sunlight, enter the darkness of my being.
Light up those bones attached to a growing tree.
Nourish the famished spirit within these branches.
Yes, I'm becoming another stranger in that forest.
Bark, root and branch, I wear the apparel of silence.

Rain has softly fallen and the soul is refreshed and free.
Yet the restive self is tethered to every part of me.
Following a lurking shadow along some winding road
I see other shades in the woods who want to follow us.
They are the sad and fleeting rags of what we will become.

Between This World and the Next

The sky is awash in faded blue and Gainesborough grey
but greyer still is the man moping along a nature trail.
Coming to rest on a bench he appears quite content
yet he finds himself in terror of a stand of leering trees.

Not one to be tempted by a sunbeam's kiss on his brow.
But he's quite enamoured with the Gloom after a rainfall
when love is in the air with its musk of earthy fragrances
in spongy moss, salal berries, algae and leafy mounds of lichen.

My psyche is stuck on a gluey net as I await that dangling acrobat.
A translucent garment of a spider's web relishes its own geometry!
Sparkling globules urge a woodland butterfly to land on-board to rest.
The spinner waltzes with his prey between this world and the next.

Their Masterpieces

A Voice in my head cried:
                'Your warranty on breathing is nearly up.'
But I'm not listening to the spook who's taken refuge in my head.
In gazing at those sprouting infants,
                I believe, I, too, can be reborn.
Standing before this gloating Douglas fir,
                I let my thoughts go free.
They slip quietly away to be nurtured
                in a bed of quintessential earth.

Those trees have eyes that see an invasive shadow
                clinging to a poet
stopping to caress branches of coral fungi
                reposed on a tree stump.
I begin to reflect upon the pet potential
                in some comedic mushroom:
Eschewing light a grotesquery of alabaster
                finds solace in the shade.
How I envy those spores of eternity
                fleshing out their masterpieces.

What's on Tap?

Poetry is a way of going out on a blind date to meet your soul, and you've promised to meet your true essence at a trendy nightclub in some dark alley of the inner city. You arrive there, sit down at an empty table, without realizing your date is sitting right next to you. It seems that you are invisible to each other. And finally this cadaverously lean waiter appears out of the shadows and says: You want to order something from the bar? Sure, you reply, what's on tap? The waiter reads out the brand names of some local brews: We have Eternal Life, a fuzzy dark cumulous of ale. We have Deep Space, a sparkly bitter beer, somewhat heavy, like a burnt-out lodestone—an acquired taste.... Suddenly you see your waiter fading away, and then it occurs to you that your date is never going to show up, and further, that you are in the wrong bar, the wrong cul de sac and even worse, you are talking to a complete stranger, your navel. That's poetry!

The author wishes to express his gratitude to 'those tall old timers still growing in Qualicum Beach Heritage Forest'.

About the Poet

Joe Rosenblatt is an accomplished author and artist who, over the course of five decades, has produced more than twenty books of poetry, fiction and non-fiction. He was the second poet to be published by the legendary Coach House Press, which released *The LSD Leacock* in 1966. Rosenblatt has since received two major awards—the Governor General's Award for his selected poems *Top Soil* (1976), and the B.C. Book Prize for *Poetry Hotel* in 1986. His poems have been translated into Italian, Swedish, Spanish and Korean. He lives in blissful seclusion in Qualicum Beach on Vancouver Island with his wife, Faye, and their generational cats, all of whom are depicted in his many drawings and paintings.